THE COMPLETE

PLANT-BASED DIET COOKBOOK

The New Complete Guide With Easy and Delicious Plant-Based Recipes All The Nutritional Needs for a Modern, Healthy, and Active Life

BAILEY PERKINS

Sommario

INTRODUCTION

There are undeniably great benefits from adopting a whole-food, plant-based diet. There are also downsides. As with any lifestyle transformation, there will be a period of adjustment and also some experiences that may be uncomfortable for you. This book is meant to help make the transition as pleasurable as possible. Before we go into the benefits, there are a few ideas that I want to make clear. First of all, as powerful as the plant-based diet is, it is not the answer to all of your problems, it is not guaranteed to cure all of your ailments and prevent all disease, and I will not bash all other types of diet in favor of this one. This is ultimately about using the best quality of information to decide what is right for your body and what you want to achieve. I will do my best to provide enough unbiased information as possible for you, and you will be responsible for forming your own opinions and making your own choices. However, don't be discouraged. Once you figure out how you're going to implement it, this eating style can help you make noticeable positive changes in your body and your quality of life. The research results from people who have adopted the plant-based lifestyle are pretty astounding. I have poured over page after page of studies and accounts where this diet has helped people overcome weight issues and have also helped to clear and prevent numerous diseases and conditions. Most lifestyle-caused ailments can essentially be improved by plant-based eating in the very least. For the most part, a healthy diet is one of the most important things you can do for yourself. We often forget just the impact that it can have. We are thinking from the outside, almost. We are the here-our body's in there; some elusive, scientific world that we don't quite understand. This is why most people just end up going to the doctor for answers and usually a new medication type. Unfortunately, this will not work if we are seeking true, vibrant health. Pills will only be a cure for some of the symptoms we are experiencing, not for the actual problem. I have been through this myself many times, as well as witnessed it from friends and family. I have had body pains that were only prescribed medicine... Stomach issues? Pills. High blood pressure? Pills. Depression? Pills. As much good as I believe medication is capable of, they are not the answer to every single ailment we could have. And many times, the side effects can be a whole other issue altogether. Sometimes, they can even be worse than the original problem, which often leads to a switch in your medication to see if results will be better. This guinea pig test can go on for quite some time! You can be left waiting for answers, collecting even more questions.

The solution I want to propose is that we take responsibility for our own bodies and learn as much as we can about the ways in which they operate. If you are going to be a guinea pig, you may as well be the scientist as well. You will know best how changes feel within yourself. Your doctor should be able to look after areas in which you need to go to medical school to understand. There is a world of knowledge that you can acquire about yourself that will go a long way toward transforming how you think, feel, and look. So let's get discussing the benefits that are available to you once you adopt the plant-based lifestyle.

One of the most sought-after benefits of a healthy diet is of course, weight loss. Most people seek a new diet for the promise of losing unwanted fat on their bodies. And although this can seem like a superficial focus, it can be an excellent starting off point. It can bring a person to a healthier lifestyle, when they might otherwise never think to look for it Furthermore, losing excess weight can actually do quite a few people a lot of good in their life.

Adopting a whole-food, plant-based diet can significantly reduce the amounts of saturated fats and cholesterol you consume when paired with reducing or eliminating animal products. This has a dramatic effect on the way your body metabolizes food-especially fats. The fat already in your body gets trapped because the food we consume usually has so much additional fat that our body must process the incoming foods before getting to our internal food storage. This turns into a cycle because we are constantly consuming food that our body must find something to do with. The natural, short-term is to place the incoming fat into storage in case we are ever starving in the future. Unfortunately, this is something that rarely comes in handy for those of us who never seem to be running on empty. The opportunity to use up our stored fat never arises because we just don't give it a chance.

In many cases, those who have adopted this lifestyle and did it properly were able to lose a significant amount of weight over time. This is mostly because you are eating more vegetables and fruit (very dense in essential nutrients and low in calories), avoiding foods that are high in calories and very low in nutrients, and disrupting digestion processes. Sticking to a whole-food, plant-based diet (when done properly) can bring about weight loss almost effortlessly. Sounds good to me!

Another one of the benefits of eating this particular diet is that you will be better able to control your insulin and glycemic levels. These two factors have an incredible impact on your health. They affect your hormones, your metabolism, and the levels of hunger that you experience.
One of the deadliest epidemics that we experience in our society is the onset of heart disease and coronary complications. For the most part, the average diet in most developed countries has been high in meats, fat, salt, and sugar. These, especially meat, fat, and salt, directly affect the heart's performance and its joining arteries. The artery walls are the pathways for our blood and oxygen; unfortunately, they can be blocked up by plaque- which is caused by cholesterol from animal meat and fat. Once our arteries are blocked enough by plaque, we are in a really bad place. Your blood cannot be properly pumped through your heart, to your brain, and throughout the rest of your body. This is no way to live. Adopting a plant-based diet has been linked very closely with the clearing and strengthening of arterial walls. Real plant-based foods can clear the built-up plaque and help to improve blood circulation.
One of the main reasons that whole plant-based foods work so effectively to lessen bodily diseases and conditions is that most of these foods are highly alkalizing. The modern diet is filled with acidic foods that, in turn, raise the acidity of the body. This creates an environment in the body that has very little oxygen. An acidic, low oxygen environment is the opposite of what we want in our bodies. This can be a breeding ground for a myriad of harmful bacteria and death for our healthy bacteria and cells. With this condition, there is usually quite a bit of inflammation, as well.

Adopting a plant-based diet is essentially surrounding yourself with live, nourishing foods. These foods have the building blocks of life that we need to survive and grow and thrive. They can be powerful allies against invaders and destruction to your body.

Basic Recipes

Peanut Butter Apple Sauce

Preparation time: 10 minutes
Cooking time: 15 minutes
Serving: 16 servings
Ingredients:

- 4 large apples (skinned, cored) 130 g. 1/2 cup
- Peanut butter 40 g.1/4 cup
- Raisins 10 g. 1 tablespoon.
- Cinnamon 120 ml.1/2 cup
- Water
- Allergens
- Peanuts (can be substituted with almond butter)

Directions:

1) Cut the cored and skinned apples into tiny pieces and add them to the saucepan.
2) Add the water to the saucepan and put it over low heat then cover the saucepan with a lid and bring it to a boil.
3) Cook the apples for about 15 minutes or until they are soft then turn off the heat and mash the apples with a fork or a potato masher.
4) Add the peanut butter and stir thoroughly until everything is well combined.
5) Add more water if the sauce is too thick, then add the raisins and cinnamon.
6) Stir again until everything is mixed thoroughly, serve warm or cold and enjoy!
7) Store the sauce in the fridge, using an airtight container, and consume within 3 days. Store the sauce in the freezer for a maximum of 60 days and thaw at room temperature.

Nutrition:
Calories: 91
Carbs: 11.7 g.
Fat: 4.1 g.
Protein: 2 g.
Fiber: 2.1 g.
Sugar: 7.8 g.

Sour Cream

Preparation time: 5 minutes
Cooking time: 5 minutes
Serving: 10 servings
Ingredients:

- 300 g. 1 cup Coconut cream
- 30 ml. 2 tablespoon. Lemon juice
- 7 ml. 1/2 teaspoon. Apple cider vinegar
- 2 g. 1/2 teaspoon. Salt (optional)

Directions:
1) Add all of the **Ingredients:** to a food processor or blender and blend until smooth.
2) Alternatively, put all **Ingredients:** into a medium bowl and whisk using hand mixers until smooth.
3) Serve the sour cream chilled and enjoy as a topping or a side!
4) Store the sour cream in the fridge, using an airtight container, and consume within 4 days.
5) Alternatively, store the sour cream in the freezer for a maximum of 60 days and thaw at room temperature.
Nutrition:
Calories: 20

Carbs: 3.3 g.
Fat: 0.75 g.
Protein: 0 g.
Fiber: 0 g.
Sugar: 3 g.

Spicy Tahini Dressing

Preparation time: 10 minutes
Cooking time: 0 minutes
Serving: 12 servings
Ingredients:

- 120 g. 1/2 cup Tahini
- 30 ml. 2 tablespoon. Lemon juice
- 1 clove Garlic (minced)
- 10 g. 1 tablespoon. Paprika powder
- 120 ml. 1/2 cup Water

Directions:
1) Add all of the **Ingredients:** to a small bowl or a jar and whisk or shake until smooth.
2) Serve the tahini dressing chilled and enjoy as a topping or a side!
3) Store the tahini dressing in the fridge, using an airtight container, and consume within 4 days.
4) Alternatively, store the tahini dressing in the freezer for a maximum of 60 days and thaw at room temperature.
Nutrition:
Calories: 102

Carbs: 2.3 g.
Fat: 8.6 g.
Protein: 3.85 g.
Fiber: 0.9 g.
Sugar: 1.2 g.

BBQ Sauce

Preparation time: 5 minutes
Cooking time: 0 minutes
Serving: 16 servings
Ingredients:

- 360 g. 2 cups Tomato cubes (canned or fresh)
- 5 dates (pitted)
- 30 g. 3 tablespoon. Smoked paprika
- 20 g. 2 tablespoon. Garlic powder
- 20 g. 2 tablespoon. Onion powder

Directions:

1. Add all the **Ingredients:** to a blender or food processor and blend to form a smooth sauce.
2. Store the BBQ sauce in the fridge, using an airtight container, and consume within 3 days.

3. Alternatively, store it in the freezer for a maximum of 60 days and thaw at room temperature.

Nutrition:
Calories: 11
Carbs: 2.4 g.
Fat: 0 g.
Protein: 0.2 g.
Fiber: 0.4 g.
Sugar: 2 g.
Tip:
Add 2 tablespoons of lemon juice for a tangier flavor, and add smoked chipotles to give the sauce some extra kick.

Breakfast and Brunch

Orange French Toast

Preparation time: 5 minutes
Cooking time: 30 minutes
Serving: 8 servings
Ingredients:

- 2 cups of plant milk (unflavored)
- Four tablespoon maple syrup
- 11/2 tablespoon cinnamon
- Salt (optional)
- 1 cup flour (almond)
- 1 tablespoon orange zest
- 8 bread slices

Directions:

1. Turn the oven and heat to 400°F afterwards.
2. In a cup, add **Ingredients:** and whisk until the batter is smooth.

3. Dip each piece of bread into the paste and permit to soak for a couple of seconds.
4. Put in the pan, and cook until lightly browned.
5. Put the toast on the cookie sheet and bake for ten to fifteen minutes in the oven, until it is crispy.

Nutrition:
Calories: 129
Fat: 1.1g
Carbohydrates: 21.5g
Protein: 7.9g

Chocolate Chip Coconut Pancakes

Preparation time: 5 minutes
Cooking time: 30 minutes
Serving: 8 servings
Ingredients:

- 11/4 cup oats
- 2 teaspoons coconut flakes
- 2 cup plant milk
- 11/4 cup maple syrup
- 11/3 cup of chocolate chips
- 2 1/4 cups buckwheat flour
- 2 teaspoon baking powder
- 1 teaspoon vanilla essence
- 2 teaspoon flaxseed meal
- Salt (optional)

Directions:

1. Put the flaxseed and cook over medium heat until the paste becomes a little moist.

2. Remove seeds.
3. Stir the buckwheat, oats, coconut chips, baking powder and salt with each other in a wide dish.
4. In a large dish, stir together the retained flax water with the sugar, maple syrup, vanilla essence.
5. Transfer the wet mixture to the dry **Ingredients:** and shake to combine
6. Place over medium heat the nonstick grill pan.
7. Pour 1/4 cup flour onto the grill pan with each pancake, and scatter gently.
8. Cook for five to six minutes, before the pancakes appear somewhat crispy.

Nutrition:
Calories: 198
Fat: 9.1g
Carbohydrates: 11.5g
Protein: 7.9g

Chickpea Omelet

Preparation time: 10 minutes
Cooking time: 30 minutes
Serving: 3 servings
Ingredients:

- 2 cup flour (chickpea)
- 11/2 teaspoon onion powder
- 11/2 teaspoon garlic powder
- 1/4 teaspoon pepper (white and black)
- 1/3 cup yeast
- 1 teaspoon baking powder

- 3 green onions (chopped)

Directions:

1. In a cup, add the chickpea flour and spices.
2. Apply 1 cup of sugar, then stir.
3. Power medium-heat and put the frying pan.
4. On each omelets, add onions and mushrooms in the batter while it heats.
5. Serve your delicious Chickpea Omelet.

Nutrition:

Calories: 399
Fat: 11.1g
Carbohydrates: 11.5g
Protein: 7.9g

Apple-Lemon Bowl

Preparation time: 5 minutes
Cooking time: 15 minutes
Serving: 1-2 servings
Ingredients:

- 6 apples
- 3 tablespoons walnuts
- 7 dates
- Lemon juice
- 1/2 teaspoon cinnamon

Directions:

1. Root the apples, then break them into wide bits.
2. In a food cup, put seeds, part of the lime juice, almonds, spices and three-quarters of the apples. Thinly slice until finely ground.
3. Apply the remaining apples and lemon juice and make slices.

Nutrition:
Calories: 249
Fat: 5.1g
Carbohydrates: 71.5g
Protein: 7.9g

Mains Recipes

Instant Savory Gigante Beans

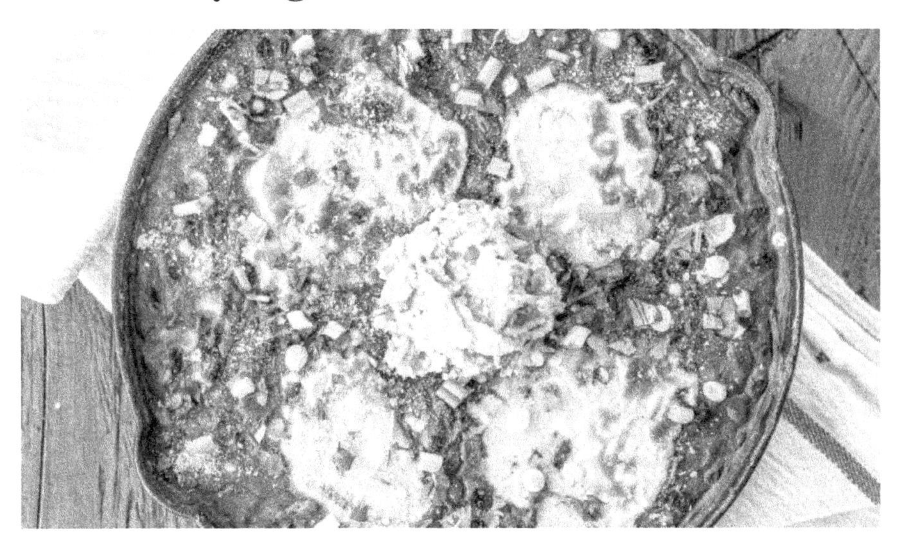

Preparation Time: 10-30 minutes
Cooking Time: 55 minutes
Servings: 6
Ingredients:

- 1 lb Gigante Beans soaked overnight
- 1/2 cup olive oil
- 1 onion sliced
- 2 cloves garlic crushed or minced
- 1 red bell pepper (cut into 1/2-inch pieces)
- 2 carrots, sliced
- 1/2 teaspoon salt and ground black pepper
- 2 tomatoes peeled, grated

- 1 Tablespoon celery (chopped)
- 1 Tablespoon tomato paste (or ketchup)
- 3/4 teaspoon sweet paprika
- 1 teaspoon oregano
- 1 cup vegetable broth

Directions:

1. Soak Gigante beans overnight.
2. Press SAUTÉ button on your Instant Pot and heat the oil.
3. Sauté onion, garlic, sweet pepper, carrots with a pinch of salt for 3 - 4 minutes; stir occasionally.
4. Add rinsed Gigante beans into your Instant Pot along with all remaining **Ingredients:** and stir well.
5. Lock lid into place and set on the MANUAL setting for 25 minutes.
6. When the beep sounds, quick release the pressure by pressing Cancel, and twisting the steam handle to the Venting position.
7. Taste and adjust seasonings to taste.
8. Serve warm or cold.

Keep refrigerated.
Nutrition:
Calories 502.45,
Total Fat 19.63g,
Saturated Fat 2.86g

Instant Turmeric Risotto

Preparation Time: 10-30 minutes
Cooking Time: 40 minutes
Servings: 4

Ingredients:

- 4 Tablespoon olive oil
- 1 cup onion
- 1 teaspoon minced garlic
- 2 cups long-grain rice
- 3 cups vegetable broth
- 1/2 teaspoon paprika (smoked)
- 1/2 teaspoon turmeric
- 1/2 teaspoon nutmeg

- 2 Tablespoon fresh basil leaves chopped
- Salt and ground black pepper to taste

Directions:

1. Press the SAUTÉ button on your Instant Pot and heat oil.
2. Sauté the onion and garlic with a pinch of salt until softened.
3. Add the rice and all remaining **Ingredients** and stir well.
4. Lock lid into place and set on and select the "RICE" button for 10 minutes.
5. Press "Cancel" when the timer beeps and carefully flip the Quick Release valve to let the pressure out.
6. Taste and adjust seasonings to taste.
7. Serve.

Nutrition:

Calories 559.81,
Calories from Fat 162.48,
Total Fat 18.57g,
Saturated Fat 2.4g

Nettle Soup with Rice

Preparation Time: 10-30 minutes
Cooking Time: 40 minutes
Servings: 5
Ingredients:

- 3 Tablespoon of olive oil
- 2 onions finely chopped
- 2 cloves garlic finely chopped
- Salt and freshly ground black pepper
- 4 medium potatoes cut into cubes
- 1 cup of rice
- 1 Tablespoon arrowroot
- 2 cups vegetable broth
- 2 cups of water
- 1 bunch of young nettle leaves packed
- 1/2 cup fresh parsley finely chopped
- 1 teaspoon cumin

Directions:

1. Heat olive oil in a large pot.
2. Sauté onion and garlic with a pinch of salt until softened.
3. Add potato, rice, and arrowroot; sauté for 2 to 3 minutes.
4. Pour broth and water, stir well, cover and cook over medium heat for about 20 minutes.
5. Cook over medium heat for about 20 minutes.
6. Add young nettle leaves, parsley, and cumin; stir and cook for 5 to 7 minutes.

7. Transfer the soup in a blender and blend until combined well.
8. Taste and adjust salt and pepper.
9. Serve hot.

Nutrition:
Calories 421.76
Calories from Fat 88.32
Total Fat 9.8g
Saturated Fat 1.54g

Okra with Grated Tomatoes (Slow Cooker)

Preparation Time: 10-30 minutes
Cooking Time: 3 hours and 10 minutes
Servings: 4
Ingredients:

- 2 lbs fresh okra cleaned
- 2 onions finely chopped
- 2 cloves garlic finely sliced
- 2 carrots sliced
- 2 ripe tomatoes grated
- 1 cup of water
- 4 Tablespoon olive oil
- Salt and ground black pepper
- 1 Tablespoon fresh parsley finely chopped

Directions:

1. Add okra in your Crock-Pot: sprinkle with a pinch of salt and pepper.

2. Add in chopped onion, garlic, carrots, and grated tomatoes; stir well.
3. Pour water and oil, season with the salt, pepper, and give a good stir.
4. Cover and cook on LOW for 2-3 hours or until tender.
5. Open the lid and add fresh parsley; stir.
6. Taste and adjust salt and pepper.
7. Serve hot.

Nutrition:
Calories 223.47
Calories from Fat 123.5
Total Fat 14g
Saturated Fat 1.96g

Oven-baked Smoked Lentil 'Burgers'

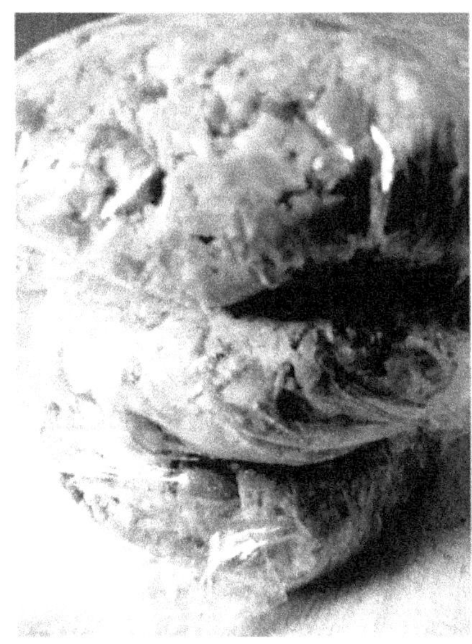

Preparation Time: 10-30 minutes
Cooking Time: 1 hour and 20 minutes
Servings: 6
Ingredients:

- 1 1/2 cups dried lentils
- 3 cups of water
- Salt and ground black pepper to taste
- 2 Tablespoon olive oil
- 1 onion finely diced
- 2 cloves minced garlic
- 1 cup button mushrooms sliced
- 2 Tablespoon tomato paste
- 1/2 teaspoon fresh basil finely chopped
- 1 cup chopped almonds

- 3 teaspoon balsamic vinegar
- 3 Tablespoon coconut aminos
- 1 teaspoon liquid smoke
- 3/4 cup silken tofu soft
- 3/4 cup corn starch

Directions:

1. Cook lentils in salted water until tender or for about 30-35 minutes; rinse, drain, and set aside.
2. Heat oil in a frying skillet and sauté onion, garlic and mushrooms for 4 to 5 minutes; stir occasionally.
3. Stir in the tomato paste, salt, basil, salt, and black pepper; cook for 2 to 3 minutes.
4. Stir in almonds, vinegar, coconut aminos, liquid smoke, and lentils.
5. Remove from heat and stir in blended tofu and corn starch.
6. Keep stirring until all **Ingredients:** combined well.
7. Form mixture into patties and refrigerate for an hour.
8. Preheat oven to 350 F.
9. Line a baking dish with parchment paper and arrange patties on the pan.
10. Bake for 20 to 25 minutes.
11. Serve hot with buns, green salad, tomato sauce...etc.

Nutrition:
Calories 439.12
Calories from Fat 148.97
Total Fat 17.48g
Saturated Fat 1.71g

Entrees

BBQ Jackfruit Sliders

Preparation Time: 10 minutes
Cooking time: 15 minutes
Servings: 6
Ingredients:

- 2 (20-ounce) cans young green jackfruit, drained and rinsed
- 1/2 cup BBQ Sauce (here)
- 1 teaspoon garlic powder
- 1 teaspoon onion powder
- 6 whole-wheat slider buns
- Asian-Style Slaw with Maple-Ginger Dressing, for topping

- Tomatoes, onions, and pickles, for topping (optional)

Directions:

1. In a large bowl, use a fork or potato masher to smash the jackfruit until it has a shredded consistency.
2. Heat a medium stockpot over medium-low heat. Put the shredded jackfruit, BBQ sauce, garlic powder, and onion powder in the pot, and stir.
3. Cook for 10 minutes, covered, stirring once after about 5 minutes. If the jackfruit begins sticking to the bottom of the pot, add in a few tablespoons of vegetable broth or water.
4. Uncover and cook for 5 minutes, stirring every few minutes.
5. Serve on whole-wheat slider buns with your favorite toppings.

Cooking tip: BBQ Jackfruit can also be made in a slow cooker. Using all of the same **Ingredients:**, cook for 3 to 4 hours on high or 6 to 8 hours on low.

Nutrition:

Calories: 188
Total fat: 2g
Carbohydrates: 36g
Fiber: 11g
Protein: 7g

Hawaiian Luau Burgers

Preparation Time: 15 minutes
Cooking time: 10 minutes
Servings: 8
Ingredients:

- 3 cups cooked black beans (see here)
- 2 cups cooked brown rice (see here)
- 1 cup quick-cooking oats
- 1/4 cup BBQ Sauce, plus more for serving (here)
- 1/4 cup pineapple juice
- 1 teaspoon garlic powder
- 1 teaspoon onion powder
- 1 pineapple, cut into ¼-inch-thick rings
- 8 whole-wheat buns
- Lettuce, tomato, pickles, and onion, for topping (optional)

Directions:

1. Preheat the grill to medium-high heat.
2. In a large bowl, use a fork or mixing spoon to mash the black beans.
3. Mix in the rice, oats, BBQ sauce, the pineapple juice, garlic powder, and onion powder. Continue mixing until the mixture begins to hold its shape and can be formed into patties.
4. Scoop out 1/2 cup of bean mixture, and form it into a patty. Repeat until all of the bean mixture is used.
5. Place the patties on the hot grill, and cook for 4 to 5 minutes on each side, flipping once the burgers easily release from the grill surface.

6. After you flip the burgers, place the pineapple rings on the grill, and cook for 1 to 2 minutes on each side.
7. Remove the burgers and pineapple rings from the grill. Place one patty and one pineapple ring on each bun along with a spoonful of the BBQ sauce and your favorite burger fixings, and serve.

Nutrition:
Calories: 371
Total fat: 3g
Carbohydrates: 71g
Fiber: 10g
Protein: 15g

Falafel Burgers

Preparation Time: 15 minutes
Cooking time: 30 minutes
Servings: 8
Ingredients:

- 3 cups cooked chickpeas (see here)
- 2 cups cooked brown rice (see here)
- 1/4 cup vegetable broth
- 1/4 cup chopped fresh parsley
- 1 tablespoon freshly squeezed lemon juice
- 2 teaspoons garlic powder
- 2 teaspoons onion powder
- 11/2 teaspoons ground cumin
- 1 teaspoon ground coriander
- 1/4 teaspoon freshly ground black pepper
- Whole-Wheat Pita Pockets or whole-wheat buns
- Lettuce, tomato, and onion, for topping (optional)

Directions:

- Preheat the oven to 425 degree Fahrenheit. Line a baking sheet with parchment paper.
- In a food processor or blender, combine the chickpeas, rice, broth, parsley, lemon juice, garlic powder, onion powder, cumin, coriander, and pepper.
- Process on low for 30 to 45 seconds, or until the mixture can easily be formed into patties but isn't so well mixed that you create hummus.
- You may need to stop the processor and scrape down the sides once or twice.
- Scoop out 1/2 cup of the chickpea mixture, and form it into a patty.
- Place the patty on the baking sheet. Repeat until all of the chickpea mixture is used.
- Bake for 15 minutes. Flip the patties, cook for 12 to 15 minutes more, and serve on pita pockets or buns with your preferred toppings.

MAKE-AHEAD TIP: You can follow the recipe through step 3, then cover the patties and freeze them in a freezer-safe container for up to 4 months. This provides you with a healthy heat-and-eat option for those evenings when you're short on time and energy.

Nutrition:

Calories: 230
Total fat: 3g
Carbohydrates: 44g
Fiber: 8g
Protein: 10g

Easy Vegan Pizza Bread

Preparation Time: 5 minutes
Cooking time: 20 minutes
Servings: 4
Ingredients:

- 1 whole-wheat loaf, unsliced
- 1 cup Easy One-Pot Vegan Marinara
- 1 teaspoon nutritional yeast
- 1/2 teaspoon onion powder
- 1/2 teaspoon garlic powder

Directions:

1. Preheat the oven to 375 degree Fahrenheit.
2. Halve the loaf of bread lengthwise. Evenly spread the marinara onto each slice of bread, then sprinkle on the nutritional yeast, onion powder, and garlic powder.

3. Place the bread on a baking sheet and bake for 20 minutes, or until the bread is a light golden brown.

Ingredient tip: If you're having a tough time finding a good whole-wheat loaf, or if you'd just prefer a thinner crust, you can easily substitute a tortilla shell or pita (here) for the loaf of bread.

Nutrition:

Calories: 230
Total fat: 3g
Carbohydrates: 38g
Fiber: 7g
Protein: 13g

Baked Mac and Peas

Preparation Time: 15 minutes
Cooking time: 40 minutes
Servings: 8
Ingredients:

- 1 (16-ounce) package whole-wheat macaroni pasta
- 1 recipe Anytime "Cheese" Sauce
- 2 cups green peas (fresh or frozen)

Directions:

1. Preheat the oven to 400 degree Fahrenheit.
2. In a large stockpot, cook the pasta per the package Directions for al dente. Drain the pasta.
3. In a large baking dish, combine the pasta, sauce, and peas, and mix well.
4. Bake for 30 minutes, or until the top of the dish turns golden brown.

Cooking tip: If you'd prefer not to bake this recipe, it can always be Prepare like a traditional macaroni and cheese. All you need to do is boil your noodles according to the package directions and then drain the water before stirring in the cheese sauce.

Nutrition:

Calories: 209
Total fat: 3g
Carbohydrates: 42g
Fiber: 7g
Protein: 12g

Instant Pot Recipes

Oatmeal with Berries

Preparation Time: 25 minutes
Cooking time: 0 minutes
Servings: 1
Ingredients:

- 1 2/3 cups water
- 1 cup quick oats
- 1 cup frozen berries
- 1 banana, chopped
- 1-2 tablespoon brown sugar
- 1/4 cup soymilk or almond milk
- 1-2 tablespoon brown sugar

For Garnishing (Optional):

- Almonds, chopped
- Coconut flakes

Directions:

1. Add water and oats directly to Instant Pot and cover it.
2. Switch on manual button for 6 minutes over high pressure. When the timer goes off allow the pressure to release naturally for about 10 minutes.
3. After 10 minutes, change the steam handle to 'venting'.
4. Open the lid and transfer the oats to a bowl and top it with mixed berries, banana, non-dairy milk and brown sugar.

Pumpkin and Oats Recipe

Preparation Time: 30 Minutes
Cooking time: 0
Servings: 1
Ingredients:

- 1 cup steel cut oats
- 1 2/3 cups water
- 1 frozen banana
- 1/2 cup pumpkin purée
- 3 medjool dates, chopped
- 1 tablespoon of buckwheat groats
- 1 tablespoon of coconut flakes

Directions:

1. Add 1 cup steel cut oats to Instant Pot, along with water, pumpkin purée, banana, and chopped dates.
2. Stir it once and set steam release handle to 'sealing'. Switch on manual button for 10 minutes.
3. Once time is up, allow it for natural release for 10 minutes. Switch on 'Keep Warm/Cancel' button and change steam release handle to 'venting'.
4. Using a spoon, mix it around. Make sure to mash banana and dates together with oatmeal.
5. Serve it topped with some buckwheat groats and coconut flakes.

Strawberries and Cream Oatmeal

Preparation Time: 15 minutes
Cooking time: 0 minutes
Servings: 4
Ingredients:

- 1 cup steel-cut oats
- 3 cups water
- 1 teaspoon strawberry extract
- Vanilla-flavored nondairy milk
- 1 cup fresh strawberries, chopped

Directions:

1. Spray the instant pot with nonstick spray. Stir in the oats and water, then seal the lid and cook on high 3 minutes.
2. Let the pressure release naturally, then stir in the vanilla milk and fresh strawberries.

Pecan Pumpkin Spice Oatmeal

Preparation Time: 15 minutes
Cooking time: 0 minutes
Servings: 2
Ingredients:

- 1/2 cup steel-cut oats
- 1/2 cup pumpkin purée
- 1 1/2 cups unsweetened almond milk
- 1/2 teaspoon cinnamon
- 1/8 teaspoon nutmeg
- 1 teaspoon vanilla extract
- 1/8 teaspoon of ground cloves
- 1/8 teaspoon ginger
- 1/4 cup brown sugar
- Chopped pecans, for serving

Directions:

1. Spray the instant pot with nonstick spray. Combine everything except for the brown sugar and pecans.
2. Seal the lid and cook on high 3 minutes, then let the pressure release naturally.
3. Stir in the brown sugar and top with chopped pecans.

Carrot Cake Oatmeal with Cream Cheese Frosting

Preparation Time: 20 minutes
Cooking time: 0 minutes
Servings: 2
Ingredients:

- 1 small white sweet potato, peeled and steamed
- 1 small carrot, grated
- 1/4 small zucchini, grated
- 1/2 cup steel-cut oats
- 1 1/2 cups nondairy milk
- 1/2 teaspoon lemon juice
- 1/2 teaspoon apple cider vinegar
- 1/8 teaspoon of salt
- 1/8 teaspoon ground cloves
- 1/8 teaspoon nutmeg

- 1/2 teaspoon cinnamon
- 2 tablespoons brown sugar
- 2 tablespoons maple syrup
- 1 1/2 tablespoons coconut oil
- 1 tablespoon water

Directions:

1. To make the cream cheese frosting, puree half of the steamed sweet potato in a food processor.
2. Add the maple syrup, water, coconut oil, lemon juice, and apple cider vinegar and puree until smooth.
3. Add more sweet potato if the mixture is not thick enough.
4. Spray the instant pot with nonstick spray. Combine the rest of the **Ingredients:**, then seal the lid and cook on high 3 minutes.
5. Let the pressure release naturally. Add additional milk to the oatmeal if needed, and top each serving with a dollop of the cream cheese frosting.

Soups

Tomato Gazpacho

Preparation time: 10 minutes
Cooking time: 2 hours
Servings: 6
Ingredients:

- 2 Tablespoons + 1 Teaspoon Red Wine Vinegar, Divided
- 1/2 Teaspoon Pepper
- 1 Teaspoon Sea Salt
- 1 Avocado,
- 1/4 Cup Basil, Fresh & Chopped
- 3 Tablespoons + 2 Teaspoons Olive Oil, Divided
- 1 Clove Garlic, crushed
- 1 Red Bell Pepper, Sliced & Seeded
- 1 Cucumber, Chunked

- 2 1/2 lbs. Large Tomatoes, Cored & Chopped

Directions:

1. Place half of your cucumber, bell pepper, and ¼ cup of each tomato in a bowl, covering. Set it in the fried.
2. Puree your remaining tomatoes, cucumber and bell pepper with garlic, three tablespoons oil, two tablespoons of vinegar, sea salt and black pepper into a blender, blending until smooth.
3. Transfer it to a bowl, and chill for two hours.
4. Chop the avocado, adding it to your chopped vegetables, adding your remaining oil, vinegar, salt, pepper and basil.
5. Ladle your tomato puree mixture into bowls, and serve with chopped vegetables as a salad.

Nutrition:

Calories: 181
Protein: 3 Grams
Fat: 14 Grams
Carbs: 14 Grams

Tomato Pumpkin Soup

Preparation time: 5 minutes
Cooking time: 20 minutes
Servings: 4
Ingredients:

- 2 cups pumpkin, diced
- 1/2 cup tomato, chopped
- 1/2 cup onion, chopped
- 1 1/2 teaspoon curry powder
- 1/2 teaspoon paprika
- 2 cups vegetable stock
- 1 teaspoon olive oil
- 1/2 teaspoon garlic, minced

Directions:

1. In a saucepan, add oil, garlic, and onion and sauté for 3 minutes over medium heat.
2. Add remaining **Ingredients:** into the saucepan and bring to boil.
3. Reduce heat and cover and simmer for 10 minutes.
4. Puree the soup using a blender until smooth.

5. Stir well and serve warm.

Nutrition:
Calories: 70
Fat: 2.7 g
Sugar: 6.3 g
Protein: 1.9 g
Cholesterol: 0 mg

Cauliflower Spinach Soup

Preparation time: 10 minutes
Cooking time: 35 minutes
Servings: 5
Ingredients:

- 1/2 cup unsweetened coconut milk
- 5 oz fresh spinach, chopped
- 5 watercress, chopped
- 8 cups vegetable stock
- 1 lb cauliflower, chopped
- Salt

Directions:

1. Add stock and cauliflower in a large saucepan and bring to boil over medium heat for 15 minutes.
2. Add spinach and watercress and cook for another 10 minutes.
3. Remove from heat and puree the soup using a blender until smooth.
4. Add coconut milk and stir well. Season with salt.
5. Stir well and serve hot.

Nutrition:
Calories 153
Fat 8.3 g
Carbohydrates 8.7 g
Sugar 4.3 g
Protein 11.9 g
Cholesterol 0 mg

Avocado Mint Soup

Preparation time: 5 minutes
Cooking time: 10 minutes
Servings: 2
Ingredients:

- 1 medium avocado, peeled, pitted, and cut into pieces
- 1 cup coconut milk
- 2 romaine lettuce leaves
- 20 fresh mint leaves
- 1 tablespoon fresh lime juice
- 1/8 teaspoon salt

Directions:

1. Add all **Ingredients:** into the blender and blend until smooth. Soup should be thick not as a puree.
2. Pour into the serving bowls and place in the refrigerator for 10 minutes.
3. Stir well and serve chilled.

Nutrition:
Calories 268
Fat 25.6 g
Carbohydrates 10.2 g
Sugar 0.6 g
Protein 2.7 g
Cholesterol 0 mg

Creamy Squash Soup

Preparation time: 10 minutes
Cooking time: 25 minutes
Servings: 8
Ingredients:

- 3 cups butternut squash, chopped
- 1 1/2 cups unsweetened coconut milk
- 1 tablespoon coconut oil
- 1 teaspoon dried onion flakes
- 1 tablespoon curry powder
- 4 cups water
- 1 garlic clove
- 1 teaspoon kosher salt

Directions:

1. Add squash, coconut oil, onion flakes, curry powder, water, garlic, and salt into a large saucepan. Bring to boil over high heat.
2. Turn heat to medium and simmer for 20 minutes.
3. Puree the soup using a blender until smooth. Return soup to the saucepan and stir in coconut milk and cook for 2 minutes.
4. Stir well and serve hot.

Nutrition:
Calories 146
Fat 12.6 g
Carbohydrates 9.4 g
Sugar 2.8 g
Protein 1.7 g
Cholesterol 0 mg

Grilled & Hashed Vegetables

Crusty Grilled Corn

Preparation Time: 10 minutes
Cooking Time: 15 minutes
Servings: 4
Ingredients:

- 2 corn cobs
- 1/3 cup Vegenaise
- 1 small handful cilantro
- 1/2 cup breadcrumbs
- 1 teaspoon lemon juice

Directions:

1. Preheat the gas grill on high heat.

2. Add corn grill to the grill and continue grilling until it turns golden-brown on all sides.
3. Mix the Vegenaise, cilantro, breadcrumbs, and lemon juice in a bowl.
4. Add grilled corn cobs to the crumbs mixture.
5. Toss well then serve.

Nutrition:
Calories: 372
Total Fat: 11.1 g
Saturated Fat: 5.8 g
Cholesterol: 610 mg
Sodium: 749 mg
Total Carbs: 16.9 g
Fiber: 0.2 g
Sugar: 0.2 g
Protein: 13.5 g

Grilled Carrots with Chickpea Salad

Preparation Time: 10 minutes
Cooking Time: 10 minutes
Servings: 8
Ingredients:

- Carrots
- 8 large carrots
- 1 tablespoon oil
- 1 1/2 teaspoon salt
- 1 teaspoon dried oregano
- 1 teaspoon dried thyme
- 2 teaspoon paprika powder
- 1 1/2 tablespoon soy sauce
- 1/2 cup of water
- Chickpea Salad
- 14 oz canned chickpeas
- 3 medium pickles
- 1 small onion

- A big handful of lettuce
- 1 teaspoon apple cider vinegar
- 1/2 teaspoon dried oregano
- 1/2 teaspoon salt
- Ground black pepper, to taste
- 1/2 cup vegan cream

Directions:

1. Toss the carrots with all of its **Ingredients:** in a bowl.
2. Thread one carrot on a stick and place it on a plate.
3. Preheat the grill over high heat.
4. Grill the carrots for 2 minutes per side on the grill.
5. Toss the **Ingredients:** for the salad in a large salad bowl.
6. Slice grilled carrots and add them on top of the salad.
7. Serve fresh.

Nutrition:
Calories: 114
Total Fat: 5.7 g
Sodium: 94 mg
Total Carbs: 31.4 g
Fiber: 0.6 g
Sugar: 15 g
Protein: 4.1 g

Grilled Avocado Guacamole

Preparation Time: 10 minutes
Cooking Time: 20 minutes
Servings: 4
Ingredients:

- 1/2 teaspoon olive oil
- 1 lime, halved
- 1/2 onion, halved
- 1 serrano chile, halved, stemmed, and seeded
- 3 Haas avocados, skin on
- 2–3 tablespoons fresh cilantro, chopped
- 1/2 teaspoon smoked salt

Directions:

1. Preheat the grill over medium heat.
2. Brush the grilling grates with olive oil and place chile, onion, and lime on it.
3. Grill the onion for 10 minutes, chile for 5 minutes, and lime for 2 minutes.
4. Transfer the veggies to a large bowl.
5. Now cut the avocados in half and grill them for 5 minutes.
6. Mash the flesh of the grilled avocado in a bowl.

7. Chop the other grilled veggies and add them to the avocado mash.
8. Stir in remaining **Ingredients:** and mix well.
9. Serve.

Nutrition:
Calories: 249
Total Fat: 11.9 g
Sodium: 79 mg
Total Carbs: 41.8 g
Fiber: 1.1 g
Sugar: 0.3 g
Protein: 1 g

Grilled Fajitas with Jalapeño Sauce

Preparation Time: 10 minutes
Cooking Time: 25 minutes
Servings: 4
Ingredients:
Marinade

- 1/4 cup olive oil
- 1/4 cup lime juice
- 2 garlic cloves, minced
- 1 teaspoon chili powder
- 1 teaspoon ground cumin
- 1 teaspoon dried oregano
- 1/2 teaspoon salt
- 1/2 teaspoon black pepper
- Jalapeño Sauce
- 6 jalapeno peppers stemmed, halved, and seeded
- 1–2 teaspoons olive oil
- 1 cup raw cashews, soaked and drained
- 1/2 cup almond milk
- 1/4 cup water
- 1/4 cup lime juice
- 2 teaspoons agaves
- 1/2 cup fresh cilantro
- Salt, to taste
- Grilled Vegetables

- 1/2 lb asparagus spears, trimmed
- 2 large portobello mushrooms, sliced
- 1 large zucchini, sliced
- 1 red bell pepper, sliced
- 1 red onion, sliced

Directions:

1. Dump all the **Ingredients:** for the marinade in a large bowl.
2. Toss in all the veggies and mix well to marinate for 1 hour.
3. Meanwhile, prepare the sauce and brush the jalapenos with oil.
4. Grill the jalapenos for 5 minutes per side until slightly charred.
5. Blend the grilled jalapenos with other **Ingredients:** for the sauce in a blender.
6. Transfer this sauce to a separate bowl and keep it aside.
7. Now grill the marinated veggies in the grill until soft and slightly charred on all sides.
8. Pour the prepared sauce over the grilled veggies.
9. Serve.

Nutrition:
Calories: 213
Total Fat: 14 g
Sodium: 162 mg
Total Carbs: 53 g
Fiber: 0.7 g
Sugar: 19 g
Protein: 12 g

Grilled Ratatouille Kebabs

Preparation Time: 10 minutes
Cooking Time: 20 minutes
Servings: 6
Ingredients:

- 3 tablespoons soy sauce
- 3 tablespoons balsamic vinegar
- 1 teaspoon dried thyme leaves
- 2 tablespoons extra virgin olive oil
- Veggies
- 1 zucchini, diced
- 1/2 red onion, diced
- 1/2 red capsicum, diced
- 2 tomatoes, diced
- 1 small eggplant, diced
- 8 button mushrooms, diced

Directions:

1. Toss the veggies with soy sauce, olive oil, thyme, and balsamic vinegar in a large bowl.

2. Thread the veggies alternately on the wooden skewers and reserve the remaining marinade.
3. Marinate these skewers for 1 hour in the refrigerator.
4. Preheat the grill over medium heat.
5. Grill the marinated skewers for 5 minutes per side while basting with the reserved marinade.
6. Serve fresh.

Nutrition:
Calories: 379
Total Fat: 29.7 g
Sodium: 193 mg
Total Carbs: 23.7 g
Fiber: 0.9 g
Sugar: 1.3 g
Protein: 5.2 g

Stir Fry

Chipotle, Pinto, and Green Bean and Corn Succotash

Preparation Time: 5 Minutes
Cooking Time: 10 Minutes
Serving: 2
Ingredients:

- 2 tablespoons extra-virgin olive oil
- 1 1/2 cups fresh or frozen corn
- 1 cup green beans, chopped
- 2 green onions, white and green parts, sliced
- 1/2 tablespoon minced garlic
- 1 medium tomato, chopped
- 1 teaspoon chili powder
- 1/2 teaspoon chipotle powder
- 1/2 teaspoon ground cumin
- 1 (14-ounce) can pinto beans, drained and rinsed
- 1 teaspoon sea salt, or to taste

Directions:

1. Heat the olive oil in a large skillet over medium heat. Add the corn, green beans, green onions, and garlic and stir for 5 minutes.
2. Add the tomato, chili powder, chipotle powder, and cumin and stir for 3 minutes, until the tomato starts to soften.

3. In a bowl, mash some of the pinto beans with a fork. Add all of the beans to the skillet and stir for 2 minutes, until the beans are heated through.
4. Remove from the heat and stir in the salt. Serve hot or warm.

Nutrition:
Calories: 391
Total fat: 16g
Total carbs: 53g
Fiber: 15g
Sugar: 4g
Protein: 15g
Sodium: 253mg

Mixed Vegetable Medley

Preparation Time: 5 Minutes
Cooking Time: 20 Minutes
Serving: 2
Ingredients:

- 1 stick (1/2 cup) unsalted butter, divided
- 1 large potato, cut into 1/2-inch dice
- 1 onion, chopped
- 1/2 tablespoon minced garlic
- 1 cup green beans, chopped
- 2 ears fresh sweet corn, kernels removed
- 1 red bell pepper, seeded and cut into strips
- 2 cups sliced white mushrooms
- Salt
- Freshly ground black pepper

Directions:

1. Heat half of the butter in a large nonstick skillet over medium-high heat. When the butter is frothy, add the potato and cook, stirring frequently, for 15 minutes, until golden.
2. Turn the heat down slightly if the butter begins to burn.
3. Add the remaining butter, turn down the heat to medium, and add the onion, garlic, green beans, and corn. Cook, stirring frequently, for 5 minutes.
4. Add the red bell pepper and mushrooms. Stir for another 5 minutes, until the vegetables are tender and the mushrooms have browned but are still plump. Add more butter, if necessary.
5. Remove from heat and season with salt and pepper. Serve hot.

Nutrition:

Calories: 688
Total fat: 48g
Total carbs: 63g
Fiber: 11g
Sugar: 11g
Protein: 11g
Sodium: 360mg

Spicy Lentils with Spinach

Preparation Time: 5 Minutes
Cooking Time: 25 Minutes
Serving: 4
Ingredients:

- 1 cup dried red lentils, well-rinsed
- 2 1/2 cups water
- 1 tablespoon extra-virgin olive oil
- 1 tablespoon minced garlic
- 1 teaspoon ground cumin
- 1/2 teaspoon ground coriander
- 1/2 teaspoon turmeric
- 1/4 teaspoon cayenne pepper
- 1 medium tomato, chopped
- 1 (16-ounce) package spinach
- 1 teaspoon salt
- Freshly ground black pepper

Directions:

1. In a medium saucepan, bring the lentils and water to a boil.
2. Partially cover the pot, reduce the heat to medium, and simmer, stirring occasionally, until the lentils are tender, about 15 minutes.
3. Drain the lentils and set aside.
4. In a large nonstick skillet, heat the olive oil over medium heat. When hot, add the garlic, cumin, coriander, turmeric, and cayenne. Sauté for 2 minutes.
5. Stir in the tomato and cook for another 3 to 5 minutes, until the tomato begins to break apart and the mixture thickens somewhat.
6. Add handfuls of the spinach at a time, stirring until wilted.
7. Stir in the drained lentils and cook for another few minutes.
8. Season with salt and freshly ground black pepper and serve hot.

Nutrition:

Calories: 237
Total fat: 5g
Total carbs: 35g
Fiber: 18g
Sugar: 2g
Protein: 16g
Sodium: 677mg

Pinto and Green Bean Fry with Couscous

Preparation Time: 5 Minutes
Cooking Time: 15 Minutes
Serving: 4
Ingredients:

- 1/2 cup water
- 1/3 cup couscous (semolina or whole-wheat)
- 2 tablespoons extra-virgin olive oil
- 1 small onion, chopped
- 1/2 tablespoon minced garlic
- 1 cup green beans, cut into 1-inch pieces
- 1 cup fresh or frozen corn
- 11/2 teaspoons chili powder
- 1/2 teaspoon ground cumin
- 1 large tomato, finely chopped
- 1 (14-ounce) can pinto beans, drained and rinsed

- 1 teaspoon salt

Directions:

1. Bring the water to a boil in a small saucepan. Remove from the heat and stir in the couscous. Cover the pan and let sit for 10 minutes.
2. Gently fluff the couscous with a fork.
3. While the couscous is cooking, heat the olive oil in a large skillet over medium heat. Add the onion and garlic and stir for 1 minute.
4. Add the green beans and stir for 4 minutes, until they begin to soften.
5. Add the corn, stir for another 2 minutes, then add the chili powder and cumin, and stir to coat the vegetables.
6. Add the tomato and simmer for 3 or 4 minutes. Stir in the pinto beans and couscous and cook for 3 to 4 minutes, until everything is heated throughout. Stir often.
7. Stir in the salt and serve hot or warm.

Nutrition:

Calories: 267
Total fat: 8g
Total carbs: 41g
Fiber: 10g
Sugar: 4g
Protein: 10g
Sodium: 601mg

Indonesian-Style Spicy Fried Tempeh Strips

Preparation Time: 5 Minutes
Cooking Time: 20 Minutes
Serving: 4
Ingredients:

- 1 cup sesame oil, or as needed
- 1 (12-ounce) package tempeh, cut into narrow 2-inch strips
- 2 medium onions, sliced
- 11/2 tablespoons tomato paste
- 3 teaspoons tamari or soy sauce
- 1 teaspoon dried red chili flakes
- 1/2 teaspoon brown sugar
- 2 tablespoons lime juice

Directions:

1. Heat the sesame oil in a large wok or saucepan over medium-high heat. Add more sesame oil as needed to raise the level to at least 1 inch.

2. As soon as the oil is hot but not smoking, add the tempeh slices and cook, stirring frequently, for 10 minutes, until a light golden color on all sides.
3. Add the onions and stir for another 10 minutes, until the tempeh and onions are brown and crispy.
4. Remove with a slotted spoon and add to a large bowl lined with several sheets of paper towel.
5. While the tempeh and onions are cooking, whisk together the tomato paste, tamari or soy sauce, red chili flakes, brown sugar, and lime juice in a small bowl.
6. Remove the paper towel from the large bowl and pour the sauce over the tempeh strips. Mix well to coat.

Nutrition:
Calories: 317
Total fat: 23g
Total carbs: 15g
Sugar: 4g
Protein: 17g
Sodium: 266mg

Curry Recipes

Coconut Tofu Curry

Preparation Time: 30 Minutes
Cooking Time: 15 Minutes
Serving: 2
Ingredients:

- 1 14-oz. block firm tofu
- 2 teaspoon coconut oil
- 1 medium sweet onion, diced
- 1 13-oz. can reduced-fat coconut milk
- 1 cup fresh tomatoes, diced
- 1 cup snap peas

- 1 1/2 inch ginger, finely minced
- 1 teaspoon curry powder
- 1 teaspoon turmeric
- 1 teaspoon cumin
- 1/2 teaspoon red pepper flakes
- 1 teaspoon agave nectar
- 1/4 teaspoon Salt
- 1/4 teaspoon pepper to taste

Directions:

1. Cut the tofu into 1/2-inch cubes.
2. Heat the coconut oil in a large skillet over medium-high heat.
3. Add the tofu and cook for about 5 minutes.
4. Stir in the garlic and diced onions, and sauté until the onions are transparent (for about 5 to 10 minutes); add the ginger while stirring.
5. Add in the coconut milk, tomatoes, agave nectar, snap peas, and remaining spices.
6. Combine thoroughly, cover, and cook on low heat; remove after 10 minutes of cooking.
7. For serving, scoop the curry into a bowl or over rice.

Nutrition:

Calories 751
Total Fat 58g
Cholesterol 0mg
Sodium 356mg
Total Carbohydrate 44.8g

Green Thai Curry

Preparation Time: 30 Minutes
Cooking Time: 18 Minutes
Serving: 4
Ingredients:

- 1 cup white rice
- 1/2 cup dry chickpeas
- 2 tablespoon olive oil
- 1 14-oz. package firm tofu, drained
- 1 medium green bell pepper
- 1/2 white onion, diced
- 2 tablespoon green curry paste
- 1 cup reduced-fat coconut milk

- 1 cup water
- 1 cup peas, fresh or frozen
- 1/3 cup chopped fresh Thai basil
- 2 tablespoon maple syrup
- 1/2 teaspoon lime juice
- 1/4 teaspoon salt

Directions:

1. Cut the tofu into 1/2-inch pieces.
2. Over medium-high heat, heat up the olive oil in a large skillet and fry the tofu about 3 minutes per side.
3. Remove the skillet from the stove and set the tofu aside in a medium-sized bowl with the cooked chickpeas.
4. Using the same skillet over medium-high heat, add the bell pepper and onions and sauté until they are softened, for about 5 minutes.
5. Remove the skillet from the heat, add the green curry paste, water (or vegetable broth), and coconut milk to the skillet.
6. Stir until the curry paste is well incorporated; then add the tofu, chickpeas, and peas to the mixture and cook for 10 more minutes.
7. Drop in the Thai basil, maple syrup, and salt, and bring the mixture back up to a low cooking bubble, stirring constantly for about 3 minutes. Remove from heat.
8. Serve with rice, topped with additional chopped Thai basil, or store for later!

Nutrition:

Calories 621
Total Fat 29g
Saturated Fat 14.8g
Cholesterol 0mg

Sodium 482mg
Total Carbohydrate 75.2g

Coconut Curry with Cauliflower and Tomato

Preparation Time: 10 Minutes
Cooking Time: 30 Minutes
Serving: 6
Ingredients:

- 3 cups Cooked brown rice for serving
- 2 tablespoons olive oil
- 1 onion, chopped
- 1 pound sweet potato, unpeeled but chopped
- 1 head cauliflower, chopped
- 1 teaspoon kosher salt, divided
- 1 tablespoon garam masala
- 1 teaspoon cumin
- 1/4 teaspoon cayenne pepper

- 2 tablespoons curry powder
- 1 23-ounce jar diced plum tomatoes
- 1 15-ounce can full-fat coconut milk
- 15-ounce can chickpeas, rinsed and drained
- 4 cups fresh spinach leaves
- 1 tablespoon Cilantro for garnish

Directions:

1. Heat the oil in a large pot over medium heat.
2. Sauté the onions for about three minutes, then add the sweet potato and sauté for another 3 minutes.
3. Add the cauliflower and a half teaspoon of the salt; sauté for five minutes.
4. Add the garam marsala, cumin, cayenne pepper and curry powder; stir to mix thoroughly.
5. Pour in the plum tomatoes, including their juice and the coconut milk; bring to a boil.
6. Reduce the heat and simmer, covered, for about 10 minutes. The cauliflower should be soft.
7. Add the chickpeas and spinach leaves, along with the rest of the salt; stir until the spinach wilts and the chickpeas are heated through.
8. Serve over brown rice and garnish with cilantro.

Nutrition:

Calories 1042
Total Fat 39.9g
Saturated Fat 29.2g
Cholesterol 0mg
Sodium 508mg
Total Carbohydrate 145.2g

Satay Sweet Potato Curry

Preparation Time: 6 Minutes
Cooking Time: 10 Minutes
Serving: 8
Ingredients:

- 2 tablespoons coconut oil
- 4 cloves garlic, grated
- 6 tablespoons Thai red curry paste
- 2 pounds sweet potato, peeled, cubed
- 14 ounces spinach
- 2 onions, chopped
- 3 tablespoons minced ginger
- 2 tablespoons smooth peanut butter
- 14 ounces coconut milk
- Juice, 2 limes
- Roasted peanuts
- Salt to taste

- 2 cups water
- Cooked rice to serve

Directions:

1. Place a large saucepan over medium heat. Add oil. When the oil is heated, add onions and sauté until onions turn translucent.
2. Stir in garlic and ginger and sauté for a few seconds until aromatic.
3. Add Thai curry paste, sweet potatoes and peanut butter and mix well.
4. Add coconut milk and water and stir.
5. When it begins to boil, lower the heat and cook until sweet potato is fork tender. Do not cover while cooking.
6. Add spinach and salt cook for 10 minutes until sweet potatoes are very soft.
7. Turn off the heat. Add lime juice and stir.
8. Serve over cooked rice. Garnish with peanuts and serve.

Nutrition:

Calories 453,
Total Fat 23.1g
Saturated Fat 15.3g
Cholesterol 0mg
Sodium 698mg
Total Carbohydrate 55.5g

Chickpea and Squash Coconut Curry

Preparation Time: 5 Minutes
Cooking Time: 4 Minutes
Serving: 8
Ingredients:

- 2 onions, chopped
- 2 inches ginger, peeled, chopped
- 2 cloves garlic, peeled
- 2 red chilies, sliced
- 1 teaspoon turmeric powder
- 2 teaspoons ground cumin
- 2 teaspoons ground coriander
- 2 teaspoons garam masala
- 28 ounces butternut squash, peeled, diced
- 14 ounces, half fat coconut milk
- Ounces baby spinach
- 1 tablespoon oil
- 2 cups vegetable stock or water

- Juice, lime
- Lime wedges to serve
- Salt to taste

Directions:

1. Add onion, chili, garlic and ginger into a blender. Add a tablespoon of water and blend until smooth.
2. Place a large skillet over medium heat. Add oil. When the oil is heated, add the ground paste and sauté for a few minutes until aromatic.
3. Add salt and all the spices and cook for a few seconds until aromatic.
4. Add squash and chickpeas and mix well.
5. Stir in the coconut milk and stock. When it begins to boil, lower the heat and cook until squash is soft.
6. Add spinach and cook for 3-4 minutes. Add lime juice and stir.
7. Serve over rice. Serve with lime wedges.

Nutrition:

Calories 149
Total Fat 2.5g
Saturated Fat 0.4g
Cholesterol 41mg
Sodium 68mg
Total Carbohydrate 16.5g

Pasta and Noodles Dishes Recipes

Plant Based Keto Lo Mein

Preparation Time: 10 Minutes
Cooking Time: 10 Minutes
Serving: 2
Ingredients:

- 2 tablespoons carrots, shredded
- 1 package kelp noodles, soaked in water
- 1 cup broccoli, frozen

For the Sauce

- 1 tablespoon sesame oil
- 2 tablespoons tamari
- 1/2 teaspoon ground ginger
- 1/4 teaspoon Sriracha
- 1/2 teaspoon garlic powder

Directions:

1. Put the broccoli in a saucepan on medium low heat and add the sauce **Ingredients:**.
2. Cook for about 5 minutes and add the noodles after draining water.
3. Allow to simmer about 10 minutes, occasionally stirring to avoid burning.
4. When the noodles have softened, mix everything well and dish out to serve.

Nutrition:
Calories: 97
Net Carbs: 2.1g
Fat: 7g
Carbohydrates: 6.2g
Fiber: 2.1g
Sugar: 1.6g
Protein: 3.4g
Sodium: 1047mg

Vegetarian Chowmein

Preparation Time: 20 Minutes
Cooking Time: 30 Minutes
Serving: 2

- **Ingredients:**
- 1/2 large onion, chopped
- 1/2 small leek, chopped
- 1/2 tablespoon ginger paste
- 1/2 tablespoon Worcester sauce
- 1/2 tablespoon Oriental seasoning
- 1/2 teaspoon parsley
- Salt and black pepper, to taste
- 1/2 pound noodles
- 2 large carrots, diced
- 2 celery sticks, chopped
- 1 tablespoon olive oil
- 1/2 teaspoon garlic paste
- 11/2 tablespoons soy sauce
- 1 tablespoon Chinese five spice
- 1/2 teaspoon coriander
- 2 cups water

Directions:

1. Put olive oil, ginger, garlic paste, and onion in a pot on medium heat and sauté for about 5 minutes.
2. Stir in all the vegetables and cook for about5 minutes.

3. Add rest of the **Ingredients:** and combine well.
4. Secure the lid and cook on medium heat for about 20 minutes, stirring occasionally.
5. Open the lid and dish out to serve hot.

Nutrition:
Calories: 334
Net Carbs: 41.1g
Fat: 11.7g
Carbohydrates: 48.9g
Fiber: 5.2g
Sugar: 7.1g
Protein: 9.7g
Sodium: 807mg

Veggie Noodles

Preparation Time: 10 Minutes
Cooking Time: 5 Minutes
Serving: 2
Ingredients:

- 2 tablespoons vegetable oil
- 4 spring onions, divided
- 1 cup snap pea
- 2 tablespoons brown sugar
- 9 oz. dried rice noodles, cooked
- 5 garlic cloves, minced
- 2 carrots, cut into small sticks
- 3 tablespoons soy sauce

Directions:

1. Heat vegetable oil in a skillet over medium heat and add garlic and 3 spring onions.
2. Cook for about 3 minutes and add the carrots, peas, brown sugar and soy sauce.
3. Add rice noodles and cook for about 2 minutes.
4. Season with salt and black pepper and top with remaining spring onion to serve.

Nutrition:
Calories: 411
Net Carbs: 47.3g
Fat: 14.3g
Carbohydrates: 63.6g
Fiber: 7.6g
Sugar: 17g
Protein: 8.1g
Sodium: 1431mg

Stir Fry Noodles

Preparation Time: 10 Minutes
Cooking Time: 8 Minutes
Serving: 4
Ingredients:

- 1 cup broccoli, chopped
- 1 cup red bell pepper, chopped
- 1 cup mushrooms, chopped
- 1 large onion, chopped
- 1 batch Stir Fry Sauce, Prepared
- Salt and black pepper, to taste
- 2 cups spaghetti, cooked
- 4 garlic cloves, minced
- 2 tablespoons sesame oil

Directions:

1. Heat sesame oil in a pan over medium heat and add garlic, onions, bell pepper, broccoli, mushrooms.
2. Sauté for about 5 minutes and add spaghetti noodles and stir fry sauce.
3. Mix well and cook for 3 more minutes.
4. Dish out in plates and serve to enjoy.

Nutrition:
Calories: 286
Net Carbs: 40.1g
Fat: 8.5g
Carbohydrates: 44.1g
Fiber: 2g
Sugar: 4.1g
Protein: 9.3g
Sodium: 42mg

Spicy Sweet Chili Veggie Noodles

Preparation Time: 10 Minutes
Cooking Time: 7 Minutes
Serving: 2
Ingredients:

- 1 head of broccoli, cut into bite sized florets
- 1 onion, finely sliced
- 1 tablespoon olive oil
- 1 courgette, halved
- 2 nests of whole-wheat noodles
- 150g mushrooms, sliced

For Sauce

- 3 tablespoons soy sauce
- 1/4 cup sweet chili sauce
- 1 teaspoon Sriracha
- 1 tablespoon peanut butter
- 2 tablespoons boiled water

For Topping

- 2 teaspoons sesame seeds
- 2 teaspoons dried chili flakes

Directions:

1. Heat olive oil on medium heat in a saucepan and add onions.
2. Sauté for about 2 minutes and add broccoli, courgette and mushrooms.
3. Cook for about 5 minutes, stirring occasionally.
4. Whisk sweet chili sauce, soy sauce, Sriracha, water and peanut butter in a bowl.

5. Cook the noodles according to packet **Directions:** and add to the vegetables.
6. Stir in the sauce and top with dried chili flakes and sesame seeds to serve.

Nutrition:
Calories: 490
Net Carbs: 61.7g
Fat: 16.4g
Carbohydrates: 70.9g
Fiber: 7.2g
Sugar: 20g
Protein: 16.8g
Sodium: 1687mg

Conclusion

We hope that this book guides you to that exceptional balance between health and dieting that you have been aiming for. You are now ready to get started or continue your bodybuilding journey, and hopefully, these recipes will assist you along the way. These will also help you reach your fitness goals!

Building muscle, burning fat, and sculpting your ideal physique is easy, especially when you go all-natural and organic; it makes things tenfold easier. It is because when you adopt a diet like this, typically, you will consume less-fortified foods with much fewer calories attached.

You do not have to live this way, and now that you have seen just how delicious and mouth-watering plant-based diet meals can be, and how easy the transition to a plant-based lifestyle can be, I hope you take the steps necessary to make the switch today. Do not be confused or disheartened by the misinformation that exists about plant-based diets. Now that you know better, you can take the steps necessary for changing your life and your diet.

It ensures not have to be difficult or overly complicated. Take it one step and one recipe at a time, and go at a pace that is comfortable for you. Experiment with the recipes and come up with some of your own. Half the fun of the plant-based diet lifestyle is experimenting with your cooking skills.

With all these recipes here in this book plus the tips given to you, I hope that you find the plant-based diet is easy to follow. Another is that meals are delicious, not like everyone is trying to tell you.

Without commitment, it will be impossible for you to achieve your set goals. Develop a practical plan that will help you transition smoothly into the plant-based lifestyle. While doing this, you should also need that your environment is conducive to focusing on your diet plan. Your efforts should be directed towards learning more about the plant-only diet. For instance, you should subscribe to YouTube channels to watch and enjoy videos of other vegans as they delve into their experiences. When making a leap from other diets to plant-based diets, anything can happen along the way. Of course, there are instances where you might fall off the wagon and turn to animal-based diets or processed foods. However, what you should understand is that it is normal to fall and regress occasionally. The transformation is not easy; therefore, forgive yourself for making mistakes here and there. Concentrate on the bigger picture of living a blissful life where you are at a lower risk of cancer, diabetes, and other ailments. More importantly, keep yourself inspired by connecting with like-minded people. Do not overlook their importance in the transition, as they are also going through the challenge you are facing. Hence, they should advise you from time to time on what to do when you feel stuck.

Cheers to a healthy life! May you find the fulfillment of your goals through the plant-based diet movement.

CPSIA information can be obtained
at www.ICGtesting.com
Printed in the USA
BVHW041404030321
601595BV00005B/152